TH[
WELL COOKED
— EGG —

Ann Carr

LONDON • SYDNEY • NEW YORK • TOKYO • TORONTO

THE AUTHOR

Ann Carr is known to cookery and food enthusiasts through her restaurants as well as her writing. For a number of years she ran restaurants in London, Wales and Norfolk all of which were warmly praised in *The Good Food Guide*. Her writing career began with Ann Carr's Recipe Collection which was welcomed with enthusiasm in the *Guardian* when it was published in 1987. This has been followed by 8 titles on gluts of fruit and vegetables.

First published in Great Britain by
Simon & Schuster Ltd in 1989

Simon & Schuster Ltd
West Garden Place   Kendal Street   London W2 2AQ

Simon & Schuster of Australia Pty Ltd   Sydney

British Library Cataloguing-in-Publication Data available

ISBN 0-671-69718-8

Design: Carrods Graphic Design, Cambridge
Illustrations: Clare Newbolt
Typesetting: Wyvern Typesetting Ltd, Bristol
Printed and bound by BPCC Wheatons Ltd, Exeter

CONTENTS

INTRODUCTION

In late 1988 the egg, one of man's oldest foods and the cook's most useful and versatile ingredient, was publicised as a health hazard. Our medical experts told us, after outbreaks of *salmonella enteritidis* in hens, that there was a chance, even if very slight, of humans becoming infected through eating raw or very lightly cooked eggs. Their expert opinion was that there is no absolutely safe egg and that there will not be one until science has discovered a way of ensuring the salmonella-free hen.

Until then it is advisable to follow official suggestions and eat only the well cooked egg, whether it is an egg from free-range hens fed on natural grains and green stuffs, such as grass; an egg from deep-litter hens which live in sheds, in colonies of several hundreds, on layers of straw or wood shavings; or an egg from battery hens which are caged and have a strictly controlled diet. How the hen is kept or what it feeds on are apparently not in themselves enough to protect the hen or her eggs from *salmonella enteritidis*.

It is important to keep the possibility of an egg carrying this disease in perspective. Remember egg consumption in Britain in the 1980s rose to average some thirty million eggs a day – eggs which came without any guarantee of safety. Until the scientists complete their researches, such a guarantee is impossible. In the meantime, and although expert opinions differ as to the way eggs can be used, it is wisest to follow the general advice that certain groups – pregnant women, infants and the elderly or sick – should eat only well cooked eggs, and that raw eggs should be avoided even by the fit and healthy.

However, many cooks and gourmets thought that raw eggs were essential to a great many dishes and sauces, so to avoid their use seems an impossible deprivation, meaning that much that was delicious can no longer be eaten with confidence. Sauces such as mayonnaise, hollandaise and béarnaise; many mousses and ice creams; the use of egg yolks as a thickening agent in soups and custards – all these uses for eggs are now inadvisable. Even an egg nog, traditionally thought of as a quick put-you-up, might put you down!

So, like the scientists, I have been doing some research, and I have found that hard-boiled egg yolks make excellent mayonnaise, hollandaise and béarnaise. Mousses and cold soufflés are delicious if made with a cooked custard base. Even egg nogs need not necessarily be based on the raw egg!

In fact, the use of raw eggs in our diet is perhaps a rather recent innovation: in cookery books over three hundred years old, I can find few recipes for uncooked eggs. It was thought then that a hard-boiled egg was easier to digest than a raw one, and that unbeaten egg whites could cause diarrhoea or fits. Indeed, the hard-boiled egg is just as easy to digest as the soft-boiled egg. And beating an egg white does help to prevent the possibility of diarrhoea because it changes the protein structure, although it does not kill any germs. Even now, in many countries raw eggs and such dishes as runny omelettes are rarely consumed. The Spanish omelette and the Middle Eastern eggah are both good examples of this.

The egg scare of the late 80s offers the possibility of a complete revision of egg cookery. This is not a catastrophe, but an opportunity to experiment with a host of old and new recipes! In this book you will find a collection of recipes for well cooked eggs which reinstates the egg as the cook's most useful and versatile ingredient.

An egg is best eaten fresh, so do not buy too many at a time. Most eggs in shops and markets are a week old at the time of purchase. Once bought, store the eggs in a dark place as they are light-sensitive and easily damaged by powerful lights or strong sunlight. An egg will keep fresh for up to twelve days in a cool room or larder, and up to twenty-one days in the fridge. Keep the eggs standing upright with their narrow ends pointing down so that the air chamber remains floating at the wide ends of the eggs. Egg shells are porous, so keep the eggs dry to avoid germs penetrating the shells and store them away from strong-smelling foods or substances. Do not store hard-boiled eggs in batches in the fridge – cook them as you need them. If using just the hard-boiled egg yolk, wrap the hard-boiled egg white in greaseproof paper and store for up to twenty-four hours in the fridge.

Eggs do not freeze whole. If you wish to freeze them, separate the yolks and whites and store them separately in sealed containers. Frozen egg yolks and egg whites will need careful defrosting before use and thorough cooking before consumption.

Avoid the lightly boiled, poached or fried egg with a very soft white and runny yolk, and the runny omelette or soufflé. This is because a soft-boiled egg in its shell or fried egg will generally have received three to four minutes cooking at the most. And a scrambled egg, poached egg or omelette that is considered at its best usually still contains some, if only a little, actual uncooked egg. This means that the cautious cook should follow official advice and offer seven- to eight-minute boiled eggs, eggs fried for three minutes on both sides, six-minute poached eggs, and no more runny omelettes.

Sauces using egg yolks to bind or thicken, where the yolks are heated rather than properly cooked, are also best avoided. These sauces – used as the basis for English Custard and many other classic dishes – are traditionally made by bringing the mixture very slowly to a heat just below boiling point, and then held there until the sauce thickens very slightly. The mixture is not boiled nor is it held at a high heat for too long in case it curdles. Therefore it often contains small amounts of uncooked egg. To avoid this it is best to add cornflour to the mixture, which binds the mixture together and allows longer cooking at a slightly higher temperature. This allows two to three minutes extra cooking, which gives a total cooking time of seven to ten minutes. However, the same care is still required in making these dishes. Boiling the mixture or holding it over the heat for too long may still result in curdling, although the addition of cornflour makes this less likely. Should you wish or need to boil a mixture, you must add extra cornflour. This will alter both the taste and texture of the dish, and turn desserts such as bavarois or a delicate cream into rather solid blancmanges.

The recipes in this book are for well cooked eggs, but they are not guaranteed infection-free. However, it is suggested that they are safer to use than recipes for raw eggs.

RECIPE NOTES
Ingredients are given in both metric and imperial quantities. Use either set of quantities, but not a mixture of both, in any one recipe.

All eggs are standard (size three) unless otherwise stated.

All spoon measurements are in level spoons, unless otherwise stated. One tablespoon = one 15 ml spoon; one teaspoon = one 5 ml spoon.

Arrowroot, potato flour or rice flour may be substituted for cornflour, for those on gluten-free diets.

BASIC RECIPES

HARD-BOILED EGGS. Many of the recipes in this book contain hard-boiled eggs in the ingredients. The simplest way to boil eggs is to place them in a pan of cold water, bring the water to a boil and boil gently for 7–8 minutes. When cooked, plunge at once into a bowl of cold water and leave to cool if serving them cold. Peel and use as required.

Shortcrust Pastry

This 175 g (6 oz) quantity of pastry makes enough for a 17–25 cm (7–10-inch) pastry case.

75 g (3 oz) cold butter or margarine
175 g (6 oz) plain flour
a pinch of salt
2–3 tablespoons cold water

Rub the fat into the flour, adding a little salt, until the mixture looks like fine breadcrumbs. Alternatively, process the fat, flour and salt in a food processor. Add the water gradually until the dough sticks together in a ball. Wrap the dough in greaseproof paper and chill for an hour in the fridge before rolling out and using.

Sponge Cake

This two-egg quantity makes an 18 cm (7-inch) cake.

50 g (2 oz) butter, plus extra for greasing
50 g (2 oz) granulated sugar
2 eggs
100 g (4 oz) self-raising flour

Preheat the oven to Gas Mark 5/190°C/375°F. Butter two 18 cm (7-inch) cake tins.

Cream the butter and sugar together until light and fluffy. Add the eggs, one by one, beating well in between. Add the flour gradually, pour into the prepared tins and bake in the oven for 15–20 minutes, or until golden and firm in the middle.

—2—
STARTERS, SOUPS AND APPETISERS

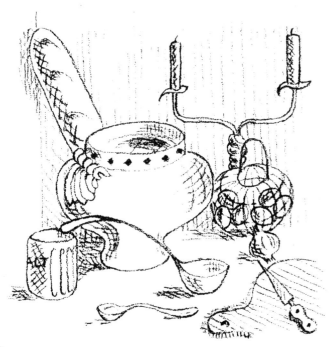

Dips are usually based on soft cheese, but hard-boiled eggs, or egg yolks, make excellent bases for dips and spreads. Soups can be thickened with hard-boiled egg yolks just as well as – or better than – with raw ones, and the hard-boiled egg whites that are set aside can be chopped and added to give texture and substance.

Starters such as eggahs – the well-cooked Middle Eastern omelettes – or hard-boiled eggs in spinach sauce, will more than adequately take the place of such classics as the French omelette or eggs florentine. The fresh herb and egg appetiser makes an unusual dip to serve with fingers of raw carrot or cucumber, and egg pâté and hot toast is a welcome change from a meat or vegetable terrine.

Egg and Herb Soup

Serves 4

A lovely soup to make in the spring when the herbs are young and their flavour sweet and subtle. It is not necessary to use the herbs given below, others such as fresh mint or savory, thyme or basil, would be equally suitable. The secret is not to use too many at a time – three are sufficient.

900 ml (1½ pints) clear light chicken or beef stock or
consommé
5 hard-boiled egg yolks
1 tablespoon chopped fresh parsley
1 tablespoon chopped fresh chives
1 tablespoon chopped fresh marjoram
2 tablespoons double cream
salt and pepper

Heat the stock or consommé in a pan over a low heat. Place the egg yolks in a mortar or food processor and pound or blend until smooth. Add the herbs and pound or blend again. Add the yolk mixture to the stock or consommé and simmer gently for 3–4 minutes. Add the cream and salt and pepper to taste and serve at once.

Egg and Garlic Soup

A soup for those who enjoy fresh garlic! Make it with fresh new garlic and serve with lots of fried bread croûtons.

2 tablespoons olive oil
2 large heads of garlic (16–20 cloves), peeled only
1.8 litres (3 pints) warm beef or vegetable stock
a good pinch of mace
6 hard-boiled egg yolks
2 tablespoons chopped fresh parsley
salt and pepper

Heat the oil in a pan over a gentle heat, add the garlic cloves and cook very gently until tender but not brown.

In a separate pan, mix together the stock and mace and heat through gently.

Press the yolks through a fine sieve into a warmed soup tureen. Slowly, a tablespoon at a time, add 600 ml (1 pint) of the warm stock to make a smooth cream.

Add the remaining stock to the garlic mixture, add salt and pepper to taste, bring to the boil and pour over the egg mixture in the tureen. Sprinkle the soup with the parsley and serve.

Cold Cucumber Soup

Serves 4

A delicate summer soup; the turmeric and egg yolks give it a subtle flavour and delicate colour. This is a thick soup; if you prefer, it can be thinned with extra milk, though the flavour will be less intense.

3 hard-boiled eggs
2 medium-size cucumbers
300 ml (½ pint) milk
500 g (1 lb) carton of natural yogurt
¼ teaspoon turmeric
1 tablespoon chopped fresh chives
2 tablespoons chopped fresh mint
salt and pepper

Halve the eggs, remove the yolks and press them through a sieve into a dish. Set aside.

Peel the cucumbers, cut in half lengthways and remove and discard the seeds. Purée the flesh in a food processor, and add the sieved yolks, milk and yogurt. Mix the tumeric with a little of the liquid and stir in. Blend all together. Season the soup to taste, pour into a soup tureen and chill. Just before serving, sprinkle over the chopped chives and mint.

Spinach Soup

A very quick and simple soup to prepare that tastes good hot or cold.

2 × 225 g (8 oz) packet of frozen chopped spinach
2 spring onions, chopped
900 ml (1½ pints) milk
a pinch of ground nutmeg
3 hard-boiled eggs
grated rind of 1 lemon
180 ml (6 fl oz) double cream
salt and pepper

Heat the spinach according to the instructions on the packet. Stir in the spring onions, milk and ground nutmeg. Bring slowly to the boil and simmer for 3–4 minutes. Remove the pan from the heat.

Halve the eggs, remove the yolks and, using a wooden spoon, press them through a fine sieve into the spinach mixture.

Return the soup to the stove and reheat gently.

Finely chop the egg whites and gently mix in the lemon rind.

Stir the cream into the soup, season to taste and serve at once. Serve the egg white and lemon mixture separately to sprinkle over the soup.

Curry Soup

A lovely, warm, creamy soup, which is very nourishing and sustaining. It also makes an excellent lunch or supper dish for cold winter days.

25 g (1 oz) butter
2 teaspoons curry powder
1 medium-size onion, chopped
4 eating apples, peeled and grated
600 ml (1 pint) hot chicken or vegetable stock (made from stock cubes, if necessary)
3 hard-boiled eggs
180 ml (6 fl oz) double cream
1 tablespoon toasted sesame seeds
salt and pepper

Melt the butter in a pan, add the curry powder and onion and cook, over a low heat, until the onion is tender. Add the apples to the onion mixture and stir-fry for 5 minutes. Remove the pan from the heat and add the stock. Halve the eggs and sieve the yolks into the soup. Stir in salt and pepper to taste. Return the pan to the heat, simmer gently for 5–10 minutes, add the cream and reheat.

Chop the whites and add to the soup. Serve at once, sprinkled with the sesame seeds.

A Very Simple Starter

Serves 4

4 hard-boiled eggs, sliced
4 large ripe tomatoes, skinned, de-seeded and sliced
1 garlic clove, chopped
a good bunch of fresh basil, chopped
2 tablespoons red or white wine vinegar
4 tablespoons olive oil
salt and pepper

Arrange the egg and tomato slices in a shallow serving dish and sprinkle over the garlic and basil. Mix the vinegar, olive oil and seasoning together, pour over and leave in a cool place to marinate for 2–3 hours.

Egg and Tuna Fish Pâté

Serves 6–8

One of the best pâtés I know. Serve with a bowl of black olives and lots of hot toast.

4 hard-boiled eggs
100 g (4 oz) curd cheese
200 g (8 oz) can of tuna fish, drained and flaked
2 tablespoons tomato purée
1 garlic clove, crushed
3–4 tablespoons mayonnaise (page 81)
salt and pepper

Place the eggs, cheese, tuna, tomato purée, garlic and mayonnaise in a food processor and blend until smooth. Season to taste and blend again.

Egg Pâté

Delicious with hot toast, this pâté is served as you would a traditional meat pâté. It makes a lovely buffet dish and is much appreciated by vegetarians.

25 g (1 oz) softened butter
50 g (2 oz) curd cheese
1 tablespoon thick greek yogurt
1 tomato, skinned, de-seeded and chopped
2 tablespoons tomato purée
2 tablespoons large black olives, stoned and chopped
1 tablespoon chopped fresh basil
8 hard-boiled eggs, chopped
salt and pepper
tomato wedges and fresh basil leaves to garnish

Place the butter and curd cheese in a food processor and blend well. Add the yogurt, tomato and tomato purée, and blend again. Add the olives and blend again. Add the basil, eggs and seasoning and blend in quickly.

Press into a terrine tin lined with greaseproof paper. Refrigerate for 4 hours before turning out. Serve garnished with tomato wedges and basil leaves.

Fresh Herb and Egg Appetiser

Serves 4

Use a mixture of any or all of the suggested herbs, for a refreshing dish.

4 hard-boiled eggs
1 tablespoon olive oil
25 g (1 oz) butter
1 garlic clove, chopped
2 spring onions, chopped
2 tablespoons fresh herbs, chopped finely, e.g. parsley,
marjoram, rosemary, savory, basil or tarragon
salt and pepper

Keep the eggs warm (if the dish is to be served hot) or plunge into cold water, leave to cool and drain.

Heat together the oil and butter in a small pan, and add the garlic, spring onions, chosen herb(s) and salt and pepper to taste. Heat through and spoon over the eggs. Serve at once.

Blue Cheese Eggs

Serves 4

Served on lettuce leaves, this makes a cool and pretty starter. You could also use this recipe to fill avocados for a lunch or supper dish. Serve with brown bread and butter.

100 g (4 oz) mild blue cheese
2 hard-boiled eggs, chopped
1 teaspoon finely chopped onion
1 small firm apple, peeled and chopped finely
1 tablespoon chopped fresh parsley
4 tablespoons natural yogurt
salt and pepper

Mash the cheese with a fork, stir in the eggs and mix together. Add the onion, apple and parsley and fold in the yogurt. Season to taste.

Pickled Eggs

These lovely, gently spiced eggs are utterly unlike those pale, oval shapes in malt vinegar which appear with some pub lunches.

900 ml (1½ pints) cider vinegar
50 g (2 oz) soft dark brown sugar
4–5 cm (1½–2-inch) piece of fresh root ginger
2 fresh green chillies
1 onion
8 hard-boiled eggs

Place the vinegar, sugar, whole ginger, chillies and onion in a stainless steel pan. Bring to the boil, cover and simmer for 30 minutes. Strain and cool.

Pack the peeled, whole eggs into a clean jar and pour over the spiced vinegar. These can be kept refrigerated or in a cool place for 4–6 months.

Anchovy Eggs

Serves 4

This makes a good starter or an excellent dish for a light lunch. The filling can be prepared in advance, kept covered in the fridge and the eggs stuffed just before serving.

4 hard-boiled eggs
50 g (2 oz) softened butter
1 spring onion, chopped, or 2 teaspoons finely
chopped onion
4 canned anchovy fillets, rinsed and chopped
2 tablespoons double cream
freshly ground black pepper

GARNISH
12 black olives
1 tablespoon chopped fresh parsley

Halve the eggs lengthways and remove the yolks. Place the yolks and butter in a food processor and blend until smooth. Add the spring onion or onion, anchovies and cream and pepper to taste, and blend thoroughly.

Fill the egg white halves with the mixture and arrange on a serving dish. Serve garnished with the olives and sprinkled with the parsley.

Smoked Salmon Stuffed Eggs

Serves 6

A delicious way of making a luxury filling for hard-boiled eggs.
Serve this starter on a bed of watercress.

6 hard-boiled eggs
1 teaspoon Dijon mustard
2 teaspoons white wine vinegar
1 teaspoon grated orange rind
150 ml (5 fl oz) single cream
1 tablespoon top-of-the-milk (optional)
100 g (4 oz) smoked salmon, chopped
2 bunches of watercress
salt and pepper

Halve the eggs lengthways, remove the yolks and set aside the
whites.

Place the yolks, mustard, vinegar, orange rind, cream and
seasoning to taste in a food processor. Blend the mixture to a
cream. Thin the dressing with the milk, if necessary, pour over
the smoked salmon and mix well.

Arrange the egg white halves on the watercress on a serving
plate and spoon the filling into the cavities – it doesn't matter if
they overflow.

Smoked Trout and Egg Salad Starter

Serves 6–8

This unusual combination of flavours makes an excellent starter, especially when served before a rich main course.

4 hard-boiled eggs
2 smoked trout each weighing 225–275 g (8–10 oz)
juice of 1 orange
1 teaspoon grated orange rind
3 teaspoons Dijon mustard
4 tablespoons single cream
salt and pepper

GARNISH
1 orange, sliced thinly
a bunch of watercress

Slice the eggs in half lengthways or across, remove the yolks and reserve. Slice the whites into neat thin slices.

Skin the trout, remove and discard the bones and flake the flesh. Arrange the trout flakes on a serving dish with the thinly sliced egg whites.

Place the egg yolks in a food processor, add the orange juice, orange rind and mustard and process until very smooth. Add the cream and salt and pepper to taste. Process again. Pour over the fish and egg whites. Garnish with the orange slices and sprigs of watercress.

Egg and Caviar Salad

A very pretty and tasty starter.

4 hard-boiled eggs
3 medium-size tomatoes, skinned
1 orange

DRESSING
40 g (1½ oz) jar of black caviar
150 ml (5 fl oz) soured cream
½ teaspoon finely chopped onion
2 teaspoons Worcestershire sauce
salt and pepper (optional)

GARNISH
a few sprigs of fresh parsley

Slice the hard-boiled eggs into rings. Slice the tomatoes into neat rings. Arrange the egg slices in overlapping circles on a serving dish and surround them with a ring of tomato slices.

Peel the orange, discard all the white pith and remove the segments. Arrange the orange pieces round the tomatoes. Garnish with sprigs of parsley.

Make the dressing. In a bowl, mix together the caviar, soured cream, onion and Worcestershire sauce. Check the seasoning and add a little salt and pepper if needed. Mix well and spoon over the eggs in the centre of the dish.

Scrambled Eggs and
Watercress Sauce

Serves 6

A summer starter supreme!

50 g (2 oz) butter
6 eggs
2 teaspoons cornflour
2 tablespoons milk
2 tablespoons greek yogurt
2 tablespoons mayonnaise (page 81)
salt and pepper

WATERCRESS SAUCE
2 bunches of watercress
15 g (½ oz) butter
2 tablespoons greek yogurt
150 ml (5 fl oz) double cream
salt and pepper

In a pan, melt the butter over a low heat. Pour in the eggs. Blend together the cornflour and milk and stir in with a wooden spoon. Cook, still stirring, until the mixture is thick and creamy. Add the yogurt and continue cooking over a very gentle heat for a further 3–4 minutes. Remove from the heat, cool and fold in the mayonnaise. Season to taste.

To make the sauce, reserve a few sprigs of the watercress for the garnish and chop the remainder. Melt the butter in a pan over a gentle heat, add the chopped watercress and cook very gently for 2–3 minutes. Remove the pan from the heat and allow to cool. Mix together the yogurt and cream, add to the watercress mixture and season to taste.

Pile the eggs on to a serving dish and surround with the watercress sauce. Garnish with the reserved sprigs of watercress.

Eggs and Finnan Haddie

Serves 8

A creamy and delicious version of this classic dish. It can also be served as a lunch or supper dish, accompanied by fingers of hot buttered toast.

225 g (8 oz) smoked haddock, skinned
240 ml (8 fl oz) milk
50 g (2 oz) butter
6 eggs, beaten
2 teaspoons cornflour
150 ml (¼ pint) double cream
salt and pepper
fresh parsley sprigs to garnish

Place the haddock with the milk in a pan and simmer gently for 4–5 minutes each side, until just tender. Drain the fish, remove and discard the bones, and flake the flesh, keeping the flakes about 2·5 cm (1 inch) in size. Reserve 1 tablespoon of the cooking liquid.

In a pan, melt the butter over a low heat and pour in the eggs. Blend together the cornflour and reserved cooking liquid and stir in with a wooden spoon. Cook, still stirring, until the mixture is thick and creamy; then continue to cook for a further 3–4 minutes. Slowly add the cream, fish and seasoning to taste and reheat carefully.

Divide the mixture among individual ramekins, garnishing each with a parsley sprig. Serve with fingers of toast.

Cheese Omelette

40 g (1½ oz) butter
1 tablespoon brown or white fresh breadcrumbs
4 eggs, beaten
2 tablespoons grated Cheddar or other hard cheese
salt and pepper

Melt 25 g (1 oz) of the butter in a frying pan and fry the breadcrumbs until brown and crisp; remove and keep warm. Melt the remaining butter in the pan. Season the eggs, pour them into the pan and cook, tipping the pan and lifting the edges until completely set.

Sprinkle with the cheese and brown under the grill. Sprinkle with the breadcrumbs and serve at once.

Cheese and Egg Biscuits

Makes 24

Crisp cheese biscuits, good with drinks or as an after-supper
savoury. Try them topped with a spoonful of soured cream or
thick yogurt flavoured with chives and fresh herbs.

75 g (3 oz) plain flour, plus extra for rolling
50 g (2 oz) butter or margarine,
plus extra for greasing
25 g (1 oz) Cheddar cheese, grated
25 g (1 oz) parmesan cheese, grated
2 teaspoons grated lemon rind
2 egg yolks
salt and pepper

Place the flour in a bowl and rub in the butter or margarine until
it looks like fine breadcrumbs. Stir in the cheeses, lemon rind
and a little salt and pepper. Lastly, stir in the egg yolks and
press the mixture together to form a ball. Wrap the dough in
cling film and chill in the fridge for an hour.

Preheat the oven to Gas Mark 5/190°C/375°F.

Roll out the dough on a floured board until about 3 mm
(⅛ inch) thick. Using a 5 cm (2-inch) cutter, cut into rounds. Place
on a greased baking sheet and bake in the oven for 10–15
minutes or until pale golden. Remove carefully from the sheet
and cool on a wire rack.

—3—
MAIN COURSE, LUNCH AND SUPPER DISHES

The hard-boiled egg has always, of course, been a popular lunch and supper dish, and the recipes in this section suggest new and exciting ways of serving them: try them hot with mushrooms, or with horseradish sauce. Instead of soufflé for supper, eggs with red peppers makes a wonderfully flavourful dish; an eggah, made with courgettes and flavoured with fresh mint, is deliciously light and subtle of flavour, and easier to digest than a runny omelette.

Eggs in Herb Sauce

Serves 4

This is a summer dish for it is best made with fresh herbs, and is wonderful served warm with fresh peas and new potatoes.

25 g (1 oz) butter
25 g (1 oz) plain flour
150 ml (¼ pint) milk
300 ml (½ pint) single cream
1 tablespoon chopped fresh chives
2 tablespoons chopped fresh mint
1 teaspoon chopped fresh thyme
1–2 tablespoons thick greek yogurt (optional)
4 hard-boiled eggs, halved
salt and pepper

Melt the butter in a pan, add the flour and blend together. Remove the pan from the heat and slowly add the milk, stirring constantly. Add the cream. Bring to the boil, stirring constantly, add the herbs and remove from the heat. Season to taste. Cool slightly and fold in the yogurt, if used. Place the halved eggs in a serving dish and pour over the sauce. Serve at once.

Egg and Avocado Salad

Serves 4–6

The creamy avocado sauce makes this salad a little different.

1 small green pepper, halved, de-seeded and chopped
2 spring onions, chopped
2 avocados, peeled and stones removed
1 garlic clove, crushed
1 tablespoon white wine vinegar
4 tablespoons olive oil
2 tablespoons thick greek yogurt
4 hard-boiled eggs, sliced
2 tomatoes, sliced thinly
salt and pepper

Place the pepper and spring onions in a food processor and blend to a purée. Add the avocados, garlic, vinegar, olive oil, yogurt and seasoning to taste and blend again.

Arrange the egg slices on a serving dish. Pour over the sauce and arrange the tomato slices on top. Serve at once.

Braised Eggs

Serves 4

This is a tricky dish, but worth trying. Serve it with plain boiled rice.

4 eggs
2 tablespoons soy sauce
4 tablespoons dry sherry
1 tablespoon olive or sunflower oil
a pinch of Chinese five-spice powder
1 spring onion, chopped
1 tablespoon chopped fresh parsley

Cook the eggs in a pan of boiling water for 4 minutes. Remove the eggs and place under running cold water. Remove the shells when cool enough to handle.

Place the eggs in a pan, and add the soy sauce, sherry, oil and spice; cover and cook over a gentle heat for 7–10 minutes. Add the chopped spring onion and parsley and serve immediately.

Eggs in Spinach Sauce

Serves 4

If you use frozen spinach this is a quick and easy lunch or supper dish; the pine kernels may seem a luxury but the flavour and bite that they add is worth the expense. Plain boiled rice makes an excellent accompaniment.

6 eggs
225 g (8 oz) packet of frozen chopped spinach
180 ml (6 fl oz) double cream
25 g (1 oz) pine kernels
1 teaspoon grated orange rind
a pinch of ground nutmeg
salt and pepper

Hard-boil the eggs, place in a serving dish and keep warm.

Heat the spinach following the instructions on the packet and drain. Return the spinach to the pan and add the cream, pine kernels, orange rind and nutmeg, and seasoning to taste. Bring to the boil, stirring, and simmer gently for 1–2 minutes. Pour the sauce over the eggs and serve at once.

Omelette and Herb Butter

Serves 2

Not the classic omelette, but one more like the Middle Eastern eggah. It is ideal for a quick lunch or supper dish, and also makes a good first course.

65 g (2¼ oz) butter at room temperature
2 tablespoons chopped mixed herbs (parsley, chives and
tarragon are an excellent combination)
4 eggs
4 tablespoons double cream
salt and pepper

Beat 50 g (2 oz) of the butter with the herbs, and add pepper to taste. Spoon the mixture on to a piece of greaseproof paper, roll into a long log and chill until firm.

Beat together the eggs, cream and a little salt and pepper until well mixed. Melt half the remaining butter in a small pan over a medium heat. Pour on half the egg mixture and cook for 5–6 minutes, lifting the edges of the omelette so that the mixture runs underneath and cooks. Finish the cooking under a grill, or turn over the omelette and cook for 2–3 minutes on the other side. Keep warm while cooking the second omelette in the rest of the butter.

Cut the herb butter into rings and place on top of the omelettes. Serve at once.

Lettuce and Butter Omelette

Serves 4

This delicious summer dish is good as a starter – serve small portions – or as a light main course. Serve with a mixed salad flavoured with fresh mint.

40 g (1½ oz) butter
1 small lettuce, shredded finely
5 eggs, beaten
a pinch of ground nutmeg
180 ml (6 fl oz) double cream
2 tablespoons grated Gruyère cheese
salt and pepper

Heat the butter in a large frying pan over a medium heat, add the lettuce and stir-fry for 1–2 minutes.

Season the eggs with the nutmeg, and salt and pepper and pour the mixture on to the lettuce. Cook until the egg mixture is set, lifting the edges to ensure that all the egg gets cooked. Turn the omelette over and cook the other side.

Pour over the cream, sprinkle with the cheese and brown quickly under a hot grill. Serve immediately.

Spanish Omelette

This version of the omelette is traditionally cooked on both sides, with a big spatula turning it over is easy. You could cook the top under the grill, if preferred. Serve with a tomato salad.

2 tablespoons olive oil
2 medium-size potatoes, cooked and cut into cubes
2 spring onions, chopped
5 eggs, beaten
salt and pepper

Heat the oil in a frying pan over a medium heat, add the potatoes and spring onions and stir-fry for 1–2 minutes. Season the eggs, pour them on to the potato mixture, lower the heat and cook until set, lifting the edges to let the liquid egg run underneath. When the bottom is firm, turn the omelette over and cook the other side until firm. Serve at once.

Middle Eastern Eggah and Courgettes

This is a Middle Eastern version of the omelette – delicious and, I think, lighter and pleasanter to eat than the classic French omelette. Try serving it with *cacik* – a traditional yogurt and cucumber sauce.

3 tablespoons olive or sunflower oil
5 medium-size courgettes, cut into 5 mm
(¼-inch) slices
4 spring onions, chopped
1 tablespoon chopped fresh parsley
1 tablespoon chopped fresh mint
5 eggs, beaten
salt and pepper

Heat the oil in a large frying pan over a moderate heat, add the courgettes and stir-fry for 1–2 minutes. Cover the pan, lower the heat and cook for 5–6 minutes. Add the spring onions, parsley and mint. Season the eggs and pour over the courgettes, cover the pan and cook for 20–25 minutes over a very low heat until the eggs are set and cooked all the way through.

Loosen the eggah with a spatula and turn out on to a large flat plate; then return it to the pan (top side down) and cook for a further 4–5 minutes. Alternatively, the top may be finished off under the grill. This is best hot, but can be eaten cold.

Eggs with Red Peppers

Serves 4–5

This dish is based on the Basque dish known as Pipérade. The red peppers and eggs make a particularly delicious combination. A bowl of thick greek yogurt and plenty of fresh bread or toast are nice accompaniments.

3 tablespoons olive or sunflower oil
2 medium-size onions, sliced thinly
4 large red peppers, de-seeded and sliced
2 large tomatoes, skinned and chopped
6 eggs, beaten
salt and pepper

Heat the oil in a pan, add the onions and cook over a medium heat until tender but not brown. Add the peppers and cook for about 10 minutes until soft. Add the tomatoes, cover and cook for a further 7–10 minutes until the mixture is very soft.

Season the eggs. Lift the lid and pour in the eggs, replace the lid and cook over a low heat for 20–25 minutes or until cooked through. Serve hot with a bowl of yogurt and bread or toast, or cold with a salad.

Hot Swiss Toast

A tomato salad is quick to prepare and complements this lunch or supper dish.

50 g (2 oz) butter, plus extra for spreading
6 eggs, beaten
2 teaspoons cornflour
2 tablespoons milk
4 slices of toast
4 slices of Parma ham
4 slices of Gruyère cheese
salt and pepper

Melt the butter in a pan over a low heat. Season the eggs and pour in. Blend together the cornflour and milk and stir in with a wooden spoon. Cook, still stirring, until the mixture is thick and creamy; then continue to cook for a further 3–4 minutes.

Butter the toast, cover with a slice of the ham each and pile on the eggs. Top with a slice of the cheese each and brown quickly under a hot grill. Serve at once.

Egg Fritters

Serves 4

This mixture of hard-boiled eggs in a thick sauce makes lovely fritters with brown crisp edges and melting insides. Serve with home-made tomato sauce (page 47) and a fresh green salad. Tiny fritters make a lovely starter served with diced tomato salad.

40 g (1½ oz) butter
50 g (2 oz) plain flour
240 ml (8 fl oz) milk
1 egg, beaten
2 tablespoons grated Cheddar cheese
1 tablespoon chopped fresh parsley
2 spring onions, chopped
4 hard-boiled eggs, chopped
1–2 tablespoons oil
salt and pepper

Melt the butter in a pan over a gentle heat, add the flour and stir in. Cook for 1 minute. Remove the pan from the heat and gradually add the milk, stirring all the time. Return the pan to the heat and stir until the sauce thickens. Remove the pan from the heat, add the beaten egg and mix well. Cook until the sauce bubbles. Remove the pan from the heat, add the cheese, parsley and spring onions, and seasoning, and stir to mix. Set aside to cool.

Add the chopped eggs and mix well. Heat the oil in a frying pan over a moderate heat. When hot drop in spoonfuls of the mixture and cook for 3–4 minutes on each side until brown. Continue until all the mixture has been used up.

Egg and Potato Pancakes with Mushroom Topping

Serves 4

TOPPING
1 tablespoon oil
1 medium-size onion, chopped
2 celery sticks, chopped finely
225 g (8 oz) mushrooms, chopped finely
4 slices of cooked ham, chopped
2 tomatoes, skinned and chopped
salt and pepper

PANCAKES
6 medium-size potatoes, soaked in cold water
for 10 minutes
4 tablespoons plain flour
4 eggs, beaten lightly
180 ml (6 fl oz) natural yogurt
2 tablespoons milk
2 tablespoons chopped fresh parsley
oil or butter for frying
salt and pepper

To make the topping, heat the oil in a pan, add the onion and cook gently over a low heat until tender. Add the celery and stir-fry for 2–5 minutes. Add the mushrooms and stir-fry for 5 minutes. Add the ham and tomatoes and season to taste. Set aside.

Next, make the pancakes. Drain the potatoes, dry and grate coarsely into a bowl; add the flour and mix well. Stir in the eggs, yogurt, milk, parsley and a little salt and pepper, and beat together.

Heat the oil or butter in a large frying pan over a moderate heat. When hot, drop tablespoons of the batter on to the pan and spread it over the base. Fry briskly for 5–7 minutes on each side. Lift on to kitchen paper on a heatproof dish and keep warm while cooking the remaining pancakes. Spread the pancakes with the topping and finish cooking under a hot grill. Serve at once.

Egg Curry

Serves 4

Hard-boiled eggs in a curry sauce have long been popular. This authentic version containing potatoes and using fresh spices is particularly appealing. The recipe is made in two stages: stage one, the curry paste, can be made up several hours in advance.

PASTE
1 medium-size onion, grated
1 garlic clove, chopped
1 green chilli, de-seeded and chopped
5 cm (2-inch) piece of fresh root ginger, grated
¼ teaspoon turmeric
½ teaspoon ground cumin
1 teaspoon ground coriander
1 tablespoon water
salt

CURRY
2 tablespoons oil
4 potatoes, cut into 2·5 cm (1-inch) cubes
2 tomatoes, skinned and chopped
2 bay leaves
150 ml (¼ pint) cold water
a pinch of granulated sugar
4 hard-boiled eggs, chopped roughly
1 tablespoon chopped fresh coriander leaves

Combine all the ingredients for the paste and, if liked, pound them in a mortar or blend in a food processor.

For the curry, heat the oil in a pan, add the potato cubes and stir-fry over a medium heat for 10 minutes until they turn golden. Add the paste and stir for a further 3–5 minutes. Add the tomatoes, bay leaves, water and sugar, stir, cover and simmer over a low heat for 15 minutes.

Lift the cover and add the chopped eggs, stir gently, cover and leave over a very low heat until the eggs are heated through. Remove the bay leaves, transfer the curry to a warmed serving dish and sprinkle with the chopped fresh coriander. Serve at once, with boiled rice.

Lentil Eggs

This combination is common in the Middle East where it is said that the hard-boiled eggs help the system to digest the lentils. Authentic accompaniments would be a dish of spinach and a bowl of yogurt.

225 g (8 oz) green or brown lentils
2 onions
1 garlic clove
4 eggs
50 g (2 oz) butter
2 tablespoons olive oil
1 teaspoon garam masala
salt and pepper
1 tablespoon chopped fresh coriander or 2 tablespoons
chopped fresh parsley to garnish

Rinse the lentils in cold water and soak for 2–3 hours.

Drain the lentils and place in a saucepan with enough water to cover them by 5 cm (2 inches). Bring the water to the boil and simmer for 30–45 minutes or until tender. Drain.

Meanwhile, finely chop the onions and garlic. Hard-boil the eggs and keep warm.

Melt the butter together with the oil in a pan and gently fry the onions and garlic until soft. Add the garam masala and warm eggs and stir-fry until the eggs are coated. Add the lentils and season to taste with salt and pepper. Toss gently and turn the mixture into a serving dish. Garnish with the chopped coriander or parsley.

Egg and Spinach Supper

Serves 4–6

Spinach and eggs are known to complement each other. Try this version of a classic dish with a piquant mustard sauce to accompany it.

900 g (2 lb) spinach
6 eggs
50 g (2 oz) butter
1 tablespoon cornflour
2 tablespoons milk
120 ml (4 fl oz) double cream
salt and pepper
1 quantity mustard sauce (opposite) to serve

Discard any tough stalks and coarse veins from the spinach. Wash well and put into a saucepan (do not add water – there is enough on the leaves). Cover and cook the spinach for 10–15 minutes or until tender. Drain well and chop finely or purée in a food processor.

Hard-boil the eggs and keep hot. Return the spinach to the pan and add the butter. Mix together the cornflour and milk to a smooth paste, stir into the spinach and bring to the boil over a low heat, stirring constantly. Fold in the cream and season to taste. Place the eggs on a warmed serving dish and pour over the spinach mixture. Serve with the mustard sauce.

Mustard Sauce

Makes about 240 ml (8 fl oz)

180 ml (6 fl oz) greek yogurt
4 tablespoons double cream
4 teaspoons Dijon mustard
a pinch of granulated sugar
2 teaspoons chopped fresh chives
salt and pepper

Put all the ingredients in a bowl and mix until well blended; then leave covered in the fridge for 1 hour before serving, to allow the flavours to blend.

Hard-boiled Eggs with Mushrooms

Serves 4

4 eggs
225 g (8 oz) small firm mushrooms
4 tablespoons dry white wine
1 tablespoon chopped fresh parsley
salt and pepper

Hard-boil the eggs, place on a serving dish and keep warm.

Wipe the mushrooms with a damp cloth, and place in a pan with the wine, parsley and seasoning. Bring to the boil, lower the heat and simmer for 3–4 minutes. Pour over the eggs and serve immediately.

Hard-boiled Eggs with Horseradish

The horseradish gives a lovely piquant flavour to this sustaining, warming dish.

6 eggs
40 g (1½ oz) butter
40 g (1½ oz) plain flour
480 ml (16 fl oz) milk
2 tablespoons white wine
1 tablespoon white wine vinegar
2 teaspoons Dijon mustard
2 teaspoons grated horseradish
1 eating apple, peeled and grated
2 teaspoons grated orange rind
salt and pepper

Hard-boil the eggs, halve them, arrange in a serving dish and keep warm.

Melt the butter in a pan, add the flour and cook for 1 minute. Remove the pan from the heat and gradually add the milk, stirring, to make a smooth cream. Return the pan to the heat and cook, stirring, until the sauce thickens and boils. Stir in the wine, vinegar, mustard and horseradish, and simmer for 2–3 minutes. Add the apple and orange rind, and seasoning to taste. Pour the sauce over the eggs and serve immediately.

Egg and Tomato Bake

This is a wonderfully fresh-tasting dish. It can be made with canned tomatoes.

50 g (2 oz) butter
6 eggs
a few fresh basil leaves, or 1 teaspoon dried basil
4 spring onions, chopped
900 g (2 lb) tomatoes, skinned and sliced
50 g (2 oz) fresh breadcrumbs, preferably white
salt and pepper

Preheat the oven to Gas Mark 8/230°C/450°F.

Using half the butter grease a 1·5-litre (2½-pint) ovenproof dish. Hard-boil the eggs and keep warm.

Chop the fresh basil leaves, if used. Mix the basil and spring onions with the tomatoes. Make a layer with half this mixture over the base of the dish and season to taste. Halve the eggs and arrange on top of the tomatoes. Cover with the remaining tomato mixture, season again and sprinkle over the breadcrumbs. Dot with the remaining butter and bake in the oven for 8–10 minutes. Serve at once.

Savoury Eggs

Serves 4

A hearty dish with strong flavours. Serve it with plain boiled pasta to make a robust meal.

4 hard-boiled eggs
100 g (4 oz) cold meat, e.g. ham, chicken or tongue
1 teaspoon capers
2 teaspoons finely chopped onion
6 large black olives, stoned and halved
2 tablespoons chopped fresh parsley
25 g (1 oz) butter, melted
1 quantity tomato sauce (opposite)
freshly ground black pepper

Preheat the oven to Gas Mark 8/230°C/450°F.

Halve the eggs lengthways and remove the yolks. Place the yolks, cold meat, capers, onion, olives, parsley, butter and pepper to taste in a food processor and blend to a paste.

Fill the egg cavities with the stuffing. Press the two halves together again to resemble whole eggs.

Pour over the tomato sauce and heat through in the oven for 8–10 minutes.

Tomato Sauce

Makes about 600 ml (1 pint)

6 tablespoons olive or sunflower oil
2 onions, chopped finely
2 garlic cloves, chopped
2 × 400 g (14 oz) can of tomatoes
1 tablespoon tomato purée
6–8 fresh basil leaves or ½ teaspoon dried oregano
salt and pepper

Heat the oil, add the onions and garlic, and cook gently for 5–10 minutes; add the tomatoes, tomato purée and the dried oregano, if used. Cover tightly and simmer for 1 hour; then season to taste, and add the fresh basil leaves, if used. Cover and simmer for a further 10–15 minutes.

Egg and Mushroom Gratin

Serves 6

A wonderfully rich dish.

50 g (2 oz) butter
8 very large flat mushrooms, stalks removed
4 hard-boiled eggs
100 g (4 oz) grated Cheddar or parmesan cheese
50 g (2 oz) fresh white breadcrumbs

SAUCE
25 g (1 oz) butter
25 g (1 oz) plain flour
150 ml (¼ pint) dry sherry
300 ml (½ pint) single cream
salt and pepper

Preheat the oven to Gas Mark 8/230°C/450°F.

Melt the butter in a pan, add the mushrooms and cook over a low heat for 4–5 minutes.

Halve the eggs and quarter lengthways; arrange them on the base of an ovenproof dish, with the mushrooms.

Next, make the sauce. Melt the butter in a saucepan over a low heat, add the flour and cook, stirring, for 1 minute. Remove the pan from the heat. Gradually add the sherry, stirring all the time, until smooth. Stir in the cream. Return the pan to the heat and bring just to the boil, stirring constantly, to thicken the sauce. Season to taste and pour the sauce over the eggs and the mushrooms.

Mix together the cheese and breadcrumbs, sprinkle over the sauce and bake in the oven for 8–10 minutes, or until the top is brown and the sauce bubbling. Serve at once.

Eggs in Onion Sauce

Serves 4

This dish is both rich and subtle; it is delicious served with green tagliatelle and accompanied by a tomato salad.

4 eggs
40 g (1½ oz) butter
4 medium-size onions, chopped finely
180 ml (6 fl oz) dry white wine
180 ml (6 fl oz) double cream
3–4 tablespoons port
salt and pepper

Hard-boil the eggs, halve them, place on a serving dish and keep warm.

Melt the butter in a pan over a gentle heat, add the onions and cook for 5 minutes. Add the white wine, cover and cook gently for 10–15 minutes. When the onions are very tender, purée them with their juices in a food processor. Return the mixture to the pan and add the cream and port and a little salt and pepper. Heat the mixture through and pour over the eggs. Serve at once.

Egg and Onion Pie

Serves 4–5

A sustaining supper dish with a hint of spice and sweetness.

75 g (3 oz) butter, plus extra for greasing
4 medium-size onions, chopped finely
¼ teaspoon ground cloves
½ teaspoon ground cinnamon
¼ teaspoon ground nutmeg
100 g (4 oz) fresh white breadcrumbs
1 tablespoon currants
120–150 ml (4–5 fl oz) milk
2 eggs, beaten
4 hard-boiled eggs, sliced
1 tablespoon chopped fresh parsley
salt and pepper

Preheat the oven to Gas Mark 5/190°C/375°F.

Melt the butter in a pan, add the onions and cook over a very low heat for 15–20 minutes, until the onions are very soft. Add the spices and cook for a further 2–3 minutes.

In a bowl, mix together the breadcrumbs, currants and enough of the milk to make a soft mixture. Stir in the beaten eggs and the onion and spice mixture and mix well. Season to taste.

Butter a 2-litre (3-pint) ovenproof dish. Using half the onion mixture make a layer in the dish; then cover with the sliced eggs. Top with the remaining onion mixture.

Bake in the oven for 30–45 minutes until the top is golden brown. Sprinkle with the parsley and serve at once.

Leek and Egg Tart

This tart is best eaten warm, you can then capture the subtle sweet and sour flavour.

1 quantity shortcrust pastry (page 9)
350 g (12 oz) trimmed leeks
75 g (3 oz) butter
grated rind and juice of 1 lemon
1 tablespoon granulated sugar
2 eggs, beaten
150 ml (¼ pint) single cream
1 tablespoon fresh white breadcrumbs
1 tablespoon pine kernels
4 hard-boiled egg yolks, sieved
salt and pepper

Preheat the oven to Gas Mark 5/190°C/375°F.

Line a 22 cm (9-inch) tart tin with the pastry.

Slice the leeks into 5 mm (¼-inch) rings. Melt the butter in a pan, add the leeks and stir-fry for 2–3 minutes. Add the lemon rind and juice, cover and simmer for 5–6 minutes. Remove the lid, add the sugar and stir-fry for a further 3–4 minutes. Remove the pan from the heat and allow to cool slightly.

In a bowl, mix together the beaten eggs and cream and add a little salt and pepper.

Sprinkle the pie shell with the breadcrumbs and cover with the leek mixture. Then pour over the egg mixture and sprinkle on the pine kernels.

Bake the tart in the oven for 30–40 minutes, until the top is pale golden and puffed up. Serve warm, with the sieved egg yolks sprinkled over the top.

Egg Mousse

Serves 6-8

This moulded mousse is particularly good with a cucumber salad.

6 hard-boiled eggs
1 tablespoon sweet chutney
1 tablespoon mild curry paste
4 tablespoons thick greek yogurt
15 g (½ oz) gelatine
3-4 tablespoons water
4 tablespoons mayonnaise (page 81)
2 spring onions, chopped
1 dill pickle, chopped finely
150 ml (¼ pint) double cream, whipped
salt and pepper

Place the hard-boiled eggs, chutney and curry paste in a food processor and blend until they look like fine breadcrumbs. Add the yogurt and blend again until almost smooth. Transfer the egg mixture to a bowl.

Dissolve the gelatine in the water over a low heat and stir into the egg mixture. Add the mayonnaise, spring onions and dill pickle and mix again. Add seasoning and fold in the whipped cream. Pour the mixture into a 1-litre (1¾-pint) mould previously rinsed with cold water.

Place the mould in the fridge and leave to set for 4-6 hours. Turn out just before serving.

Egg and Prawn Mould

Serves 12–14

A party piece!

> 6 hard-boiled eggs, chopped
> 450 g (1 lb) peeled prawns
> 225 g (8 oz) cooked green peas
> 225 g (8 oz) cooked diced carrots
> 1 dill pickle, chopped very finely
> 1 spring onion, chopped very finely
> 1 tablespoon chopped fresh parsley
> 2 tablespoons chopped fresh mint
> 300 ml (½ pint) mayonnaise (page 81)
> 4 tablespoons greek yogurt
> 11 g (0·4 oz) sachet of gelatine
> 4 tablespoons dry white wine
> salt and pepper

Mix together the eggs, prawns, peas, carrots, dill pickle, spring onion and herbs in a large bowl.

In a separate bowl mix together the mayonnaise and yogurt.

In a saucepan, sprinkle the gelatine over the white wine and heat very gently until dissolved. Remove the pan from the heat and cool slightly. Add a tablespoon of the mayonnaise and yogurt mixture to the dissolved gelatine (do not add the gelatine to the mayonnaise mixture, the gelatine may set at once and form lumps). Then stir the gelatine mixture into the remaining mayonnaise and yogurt mixture. Season well.

Pour the yogurt mixture over the egg and prawn mixture and fold in carefully. Spoon the mixture into a 1·8-litre (3-pint) mould previously rinsed in cold water. Press down well and leave to set in the fridge for 4–6 hours.

NOTE
If a firmer mould is desired, add an extra teaspoon of gelatine.

Egg and Cheese Fondue

The addition of cornflour allows you to cook the fondue for longer, so helping to ensure that the eggs are properly cooked. It is based upon a fondue originating in the Jura district in France which, unlike many Swiss versions, contains eggs, and so is much easier to digest. Serve with cubes of fresh French bread.

300 ml (½ pint) white wine
2 garlic cloves, halved
40 g (1½ oz) butter
6 eggs, beaten
225 g (8 oz) Gruyère cheese
1 tablespoon cornflour
a pinch of ground nutmeg
salt and pepper

Heat the wine in a saucepan with the garlic, bring to the boil and boil vigorously until it is reduced by half. Strain the liquid and leave to cool.

In a fondue or small heavy-bottomed pan, melt the butter over a gentle heat. Add the eggs, cheese and half the wine mixture. Mix the cornflour to a smooth paste with the remaining wine and stir into the egg mixture. Season with the nutmeg and salt and pepper to taste.

Cook over a low heat, stirring all the time, until the mixture becomes thick and creamy and bubbles round the edges.

French Beans with Eggs

Serves 4

Adding chopped hard-boiled eggs turns plain boiled or steamed beans into a special accompaniment.

450 g (1 lb) french beans
2 hard-boiled eggs, chopped
2 spring onions, chopped
25 g (1 oz) butter
salt and pepper

Steam or cook the beans in boiling, salted water until just tender. Drain well. Stir in the eggs and spring onions and the butter until it is melted, and season with salt and pepper.

−4−

DESSERTS,
PUDDINGS AND ICES

C reams and mousses, parfaits and ices are more often than
not based on a raw egg mixture using either lightly cooked
egg yolks as a thickening agent or whipped egg whites to lighten
a rich basic mixture. Although it may no longer be advisable to
use these mixtures, clever cooks need not worry, for there is a
host of delicious and exciting recipes for desserts, creams and
ices using a well-cooked egg base. Try maple cream, lemon
soufflé or rich frozen custard cream, to name but a few.

Buttered Pears in Vanilla Sauce

Serves 4–5

A lovely hot dish for late summer or early autumn.

5 pears
100 g (4 oz) soft light brown sugar
50 g (2 oz) butter

VANILLA SAUCE
1 teaspoon cornflour
300 ml (½ pint) creamy milk
2 egg yolks, beaten
2 teaspoons granulated sugar
a few drops of vanilla extract or essence

Preheat the oven to Gas Mark 7/220°C/425°F.

Peel and slice the pears, place in a shallow baking dish, sprinkle with the soft brown sugar, and dot with the butter. Bake for 15–20 minutes in the oven until brown on top.

Meanwhile, make the sauce. Mix the cornflour with a tablespoon of the milk and heat the remainder of the milk in a pan. Add the cornflour mixture to the hot milk and bring to the boil, stirring. Remove the pan from the heat; then add the egg yolks and granulated sugar. Reheat over a low heat. Cook for 3–4 minutes, stir in the vanilla extract or essence and pour over the hot pears.

Apples in Batter

Apple-in-the-hole instead of sausages! Rum-flavoured apples in crispy sweet batter make a delicious dessert. Serve with a bowl of whipped cream.

450 g (1 lb) eating apples
2 tablespoons rum
25 g (1 oz) butter for greasing
225 g (8 oz) plain flour
2 eggs
2 tablespoons caster sugar
300 ml (½ pint) milk

Preheat the oven to Gas Mark 5/190°C/375°F.

Peel and core the apples, slice into rings and toss in the rum. Generously grease a shallow ovenproof dish with the butter. Arrange the apple slices in the dish.

Place the flour in a bowl, drop in the eggs, add the sugar and milk and beat until smooth.

Pour the batter over the apple slices and bake for 45 minutes in the oven.

Lemon Soufflé

This version of a lemon soufflé is light, but well cooked. It contains slightly more lemon than usual and is refreshingly sharp. Serve with single cream and caster sugar.

50 g (2 oz) butter, plus extra for greasing
40 g (1½ oz) plain flour
300 ml (½ pint) milk
2 teaspoons cornflour
juice and grated rind of 2 lemons
75 g (3 oz) caster sugar
3 eggs, separated, plus 1 egg white

Preheat the oven to Gas Mark 7/220°C/425°F.

Grease a soufflé dish with butter, butter some greaseproof paper and tie a band round the dish so it stands above the rim.

Melt the butter in a pan, add the flour, cook for 1 minute and remove from the heat. Gradually stir in the milk, return the pan to the heat and cook, stirring constantly, until the sauce thickens.

Mix the cornflour with the lemon juice and add to the sauce. Stir in the grated lemon rind and the sugar. Stirring constantly, cook until the sauce thickens again and begins to boil. Remove the pan from the heat and beat in the egg yolks. Cool. Beat the egg whites until stiff and then fold in.

Pour the mixture into the prepared soufflé dish and bake in the oven for 15–20 minutes until well risen and firm in the middle.

Lime Tart

Serves 4–5

A crisp pastry case filled with a creamy and refreshing filling.

1 quantity shortcrust pastry (page 9)
grated rind and juice of 3 limes
100 g (4 oz) caster sugar
50 g (2 oz) butter
4 eggs, beaten

Line a 20 cm (8-inch) pie dish with the pastry. Chill.

Put the rind and juice of the limes in a saucepan, add the sugar and butter and, over a low heat, cook until the butter has melted and the sugar dissolved. Add the eggs and cook to heat through. Do not boil. Remove the pan from the heat and cool.

Preheat the oven to Gas Mark 4/180°C/350°F.

When quite cold, pour the lime mixture into the pastry case and bake in the oven for 20–30 minutes until the pastry is golden and the filling set.

Baked Custard

Serves 4

This is a great favourite of mine. To ensure it is well cooked, it is gently precooked with cornflour before baking. This rich custard may be used in place of a crème brulée.

600 ml (1 pint) single cream
2 teaspoons cornflour
50 g (2 oz) caster sugar
4 eggs, beaten
a few drops of vanilla extract or essence
butter for greasing

Preheat the oven to Gas Mark 3/160°C/325°F

Gently heat the cream in a pan. In a bowl, mix together the cornflour and sugar with a little of the warm cream. Stir in the beaten eggs, sugar mixture, vanilla extract or essence and the remaining warm cream. Pour the mixture into the pan. Over a very low heat, stirring constantly, cook the custard until it just coats the back of a spoon – on no account let the mixture boil.

Pour the custard into a well-buttered 1·2-litre (2-pint) ovenproof dish and bake for 1 hour. Serve warm or chilled.

VARIATION
To brulée the custard, sprinkle the top of the cold custard with 2 tablespoons of caster sugar and place the dish under a hot grill to brown the surface – the sugar should bubble and caramelise. (Take care: sugar burns easily.) Chill well before serving.

Orange Custard

This simple dessert is delightfully refreshing.

4 oranges
1 tablespoon orange liqueur
1 teaspoon chopped fresh mint
50 g (2 oz) caster sugar
1 tablespoon cornflour
600 ml (1 pint) creamy milk, or a mixture of half milk
and half cream
4 egg yolks, beaten
25 g (1 oz) granulated sugar
a few mint leaves to decorate

Using a sharp knife, peel the rind and white pith from the oranges; then slice across into thin rings. Arrange in a serving dish and sprinkle with the liqueur, chopped mint and caster sugar.

Mix the cornflour to a smooth paste with 2 tablespoons of the milk or milk and cream mixture. Heat the remaining milk or milk and cream in a pan, stir in the cornflour mixture, the beaten egg yolks and the granulated sugar and, over a gentle heat, cook until the mixture thickens. Cook for a further 2–3 minutes. Remove the pan from the heat and, stirring to prevent a skin forming, cool slightly. Pour over the orange slices. Chill for 2–3 hours. Serve decorated with mint leaves.

A Rhubarb Tansy

Tansy is an old-fashioned pudding made with apples and
thickened with egg yolks, and traditionally flavoured with the
dark green, bitter herb, tansy. Often nowadays, however, the
name refers to a thickened fruit pudding which does not have to
contain tansy itself.

450 g (1 lb) trimmed rhubarb
50 g (2 oz) butter
juice and grated rind of 1 orange
100 g (4 oz) granulated sugar
4 egg yolks
1 teaspoon cornflour
4 tablespoons single cream

Chop the rhubarb into short pieces and place in a pan with the
butter and the orange juice. Bring to the boil over a low heat,
cover tightly and cook for 10–15 minutes until tender. Remove
the pan from the heat, mash with a fork and add the sugar and
the orange rind.

Beat the egg yolks in a bowl. Mix the cornflour and the cream
together until smooth, stir into the yolks and pour over the
rhubarb. Return the pan to the heat and, stirring constantly, cook
slowly until the mixture thickens. Pour the tansy into a serving
dish, cool and chill before serving.

Gooseberry Fool

A lovely summer dessert using well cooked eggs to thicken the fool as well as whipped cream.

675 g (1½ lb) green gooseberries
25 g (1 oz) butter
4 tablespoons sweet white wine
2 teaspoons cornflour
300 ml (½ pint) milk
3 eggs, beaten
150 ml (5 fl oz) double cream

Top and tail, and wash and drain the gooseberries. Place them in a saucepan with the butter and wine and bring to the boil. Lower the heat, cover and simmer gently until soft and mushy, taking care that they don't dry out.

Pour the mixture into a food processor and blend until smooth.

Mix the cornflour with the milk, add the beaten eggs and pour into a pan. Cook over a very low heat, stirring constantly with a wooden spoon, until smooth and thickened. Cook for a further 2–3 minutes and then remove from the heat. Stir in the gooseberry purée and leave to cool.

When quite cold fold in the whipped cream. Chill and serve with sponge fingers.

Cold Syllabub Queen

Serves 4–5

A cold version of the classic Queen of Puddings, substituting an old English syllabub for the traditional soft meringue topping. Prepare several hours in advance, making the base first, and assemble just before serving.

BASE
150 g (5 oz) cake crumbs (page 9)
25 g (1 oz) caster sugar
grated rind of 1 lemon
600 ml (1 pint) creamy milk
50 g (2 oz) butter, plus extra for greasing
4 egg yolks, beaten
2 tablespoons raspberry jam

SYLLABUB TOPPING
150 ml (¼ pint) dry sherry
juice of 1 lemon
1 teaspoon grated orange rind
50 g (2 oz) caster sugar
300 ml (½ pint) double cream

Preheat the oven to Gas Mark 4/180°C/350°F.

To make the base, place the cake crumbs, sugar and lemon rind in a bowl. Heat the milk and butter until the butter melts and pour over the cake crumbs. Leave to stand for 10 minutes.

Add the egg yolks to the milk mixture, stir well and pour into a well-buttered 1·2-litre (2-pint) ovenproof dish. Stand the dish in a pan of warm water and bake for 30–40 minutes or until firm.

Remove the dish from the oven, cool and chill.

Meanwhile, make the topping. Pour the sherry into a bowl; then add the lemon juice, orange rind and sugar. Pour in the cream and beat with a hand whisk or an electric beater until thick. Chill for 2–3 hours.

Just before serving, spread the custard base with the jam; then top with the syllabub topping.

Lemon Chiffon Layer

Serves 4-6

A lovely bitter-sweet combination.

300 ml (½ pint) water
50 g (2 oz) cornflour
juice and grated rind of 2 lemons
75 g (3 oz) butter
100 g (4 oz) granulated sugar
4 egg yolks, beaten
100 g (4 oz) finely crushed sweet biscuits, e.g.
digestives or shortbread
1 teaspoon ground cinnamon
150 ml (¼ pint) double cream
2 tablespoons dark rum

Pour the water into a pan. Mix the cornflour with the lemon juice to make a smooth paste and stir into the water. Add the grated lemon rind, 50 g (2 oz) of the butter and the sugar. Over a low heat cook, stirring continuously with a wooden spoon, until the mixture thickens and boils. Remove the pan from the heat, add a tablespoon of the mixture to the egg yolks and return this mixture to the pan. Return to the heat and cook gently until the mixture starts to simmer; then cook for 2–3 minutes. Remove the pan from the heat and cool. Stir occasionally to prevent a skin forming.

Meanwhile, mix together the crushed biscuits and the cinnamon. Melt the remaining butter and stir it into the biscuit mixture. Mix well.

Place the double cream in another bowl, add the rum and beat until thick.

In individual glasses layer the biscuit mixture with the lemon mixture, finishing with a lemon layer. Top this with the rum-flavoured whipped cream. Serve chilled.

Lemon Marshmallow Mousse

Serves 4

A light and fluffy dessert. It is essential to use a home-made lemon curd (page 93).

2 teaspoons gelatine
2 tablespoons water
grated rind and juice of 1 lemon
2 tablespoons dry sherry
18 white marshmallows, cut into small pieces
4 tablespoons lemon curd (page 93)
150 ml (¼ pint) double cream, whipped

Sprinkle the gelatine over the water in a pan placed over a low heat. Stir until the gelatine is dissolved. Add the lemon rind and juice.

Pour the sherry into a pan, heat gently and add the marshmallows, letting them melt but not dissolve completely. Remove the pan from the heat, add the lemon and gelatine mixture, mix well and cool.

Fold the lemon curd and whipped cream into the cooled mixture and then pour it into a serving dish. Chill for 2–3 hours before serving.

Chocolate Marquise Cream

Serves 6–8

A true chocolate mousse is made with raw eggs, this dense and delicious chocolate marquise is to me infinitely preferable. Make it the day before you intend to serve it.

> *2 teaspoons cornflour*
> *150 ml (¼ pint) milk*
> *5 egg yolks, beaten*
> *275 g (10 oz) plain dark chocolate, broken into pieces*
> *100 g (4 oz) unsalted butter, cut into small pieces*
> *450 ml (15 fl oz) double cream, whipped*

Mix together the cornflour and milk, add the egg yolks and mix well. Pour into a double boiler or a bowl placed over a pan of hot water and cook until thick. Cook for a further 3–4 minutes. Remove from the heat and cool slightly.

Add the chocolate pieces and stir until melted. Using a rotary whisk or an electric mixer, beat in the butter and then continue beating until the mixture is light and fluffy. When just warm, fold in the whipped cream. Pour the mixture into a serving dish and chill in the refrigerator overnight.

Chocolate Cherry Pudding

Serves 6

A dessert with a lovely texture of nuts and cake crumbs. Start the preparation the day before you want to eat it.

100 g (4 oz) glacé cherries
4 tablespoons white rum or kirsch
50 g (2 oz) walnuts, chopped finely
175 g (6 oz) cake crumbs (page 9)
2 teaspoons cornflour
600 ml (1 pint) creamy milk
5 egg yolks, beaten
175 g (6 oz) plain dark chocolate, broken into pieces
a little whipped cream and a few glacé cherries
to decorate

Rinse the cherries to remove the sticky syrup, pat dry on kitchen paper, halve and place in a screw-topped jar. Pour over the alcohol and leave for at least 24 hours, shaking occasionally, to absorb the flavour.

Next day mix together the nuts and cake crumbs.

Mix the cornflour to a smooth paste with 2 tablespoons of the milk and heat the remainder in a pan. Add the cornflour mixture to the egg yolks, mix well and pour into the warm milk. Stirring constantly, cook over a low heat until the mixture thickens. Cook for a further 2–3 minutes. Remove the pan from the heat and cool slightly. Add the chocolate pieces, stirring until they have dissolved. Cool until the mixture is just warm.

Fold in the nut and cake crumb mixture and the cherries with their juices. Pour the mixture into a serving dish and chill for 3–4 hours. Serve decorated with whipped cream and glacé cherries.

Rum Cream and Chocolate Mould

Serves 6–8

A rich dark chocolate dessert covered with a velvety smooth rum sauce. Start making it well in advance.

450 g (1 lb) curd cheese
50 g (2 oz) caster sugar
50 g (2 oz) butter
275 g (10 oz) plain dark chocolate, broken into pieces
150 ml (¼ pint) double cream, whipped
2 teaspoons gelatine, dissolved in 2 tablespoons hot water
½ teaspoon cocoa powder

RUM SAUCE
225 g (8 oz) caster sugar
4 tablespoons water
4 egg yolks
300 ml (½ pint) double cream
1 tablespoon dark rum

Place the curd cheese in a food processor and blend until smooth. Add the sugar.

Place the butter and the chocolate in a saucepan and allow to melt over a very low heat. Cool. Stir into the cheese mixture with the cream. Check that the gelatine has dissolved and add it to the cheese and chocolate mixture. Process until light and fluffy.

Rinse a 900 ml (1½-pint) bowl or mould with cold water, pour in the chocolate mixture and leave to set for 4–6 hours (preferably overnight).

To make the sauce, dissolve the sugar in the water over a very low heat. When the sugar has dissolved, boil the syrup for 2–3 minutes. Remove the pan from the heat.

Whip the egg yolks until pale and fluffy; then pour on the hot sugar syrup, beating all the time. Return the mixture to the pan, add the cream and bring very slowly to the boil, stirring all the time. Simmer for 1–2 minutes and remove from the heat. Add the rum, strain and cool.

Turn out the chocolate pudding on to a large serving dish – best done by heating a knife in boiling water and running it round the inside of the bowl beforehand. Pour the rum sauce over the pudding; then chill for 1–2 hours. Just before serving, dust with the cocoa powder.

Almond Cream

Serves 4–5

A real delight!

2 teaspoons cornflour
300 ml (½ pint) milk
4 egg yolks
50 g (2 oz) caster sugar
2 teaspoons gelatine
2 tablespoons dry white wine
5 pairs of Italian amaretti biscuits or macaroons,
crushed
150 ml (¼ pint) double cream, whipped

Mix the cornflour with the milk and pour into a pan. Beat the egg yolks with the sugar until pale. Add this mixture to the pan. Cook the mixture over a low heat until it begins to thicken. Cook for a further 2–3 minutes. Remove the pan from the heat and cool, stirring occasionally to prevent a skin forming.

Mix the gelatine with the white wine in a pan and dissolve over a low heat.

When the egg mixture is cool, add the gelatine mixture, stirring well. Pour the 'cream' into a bowl, cool thoroughly and, when the mixture is just beginning to set, add the crushed biscuits and fold in the whipped cream. Pour into a serving dish and leave to set.

Maple Syrup Cream

Serves 6–8

Maple syrup gives a wonderful flavour to this velvety cream which is smooth and rich. Serve small helpings of it with ginger biscuits.

300 ml (½ pint) maple syrup
4 egg yolks, beaten
2 teaspoons cornflour
2 tablespoons water
600 ml (1 pint) double cream, whipped
a few drops of vanilla extract or essence

Heat the syrup and, when almost boiling, pour it on to the egg yolks in a slow stream, beating continuously. Mix the cornflour and water together to make a smooth cream and add to the egg yolk mixture. Place the pan over a very low heat, bring just to the boil, simmer for 2 minutes, remove from the heat and cool. Stir occasionally to prevent a skin forming.

When cool, fold in the whipped double cream and the vanilla extract or essence. Chill for 2 hours before serving in small individual dishes.

Frozen Custard Cream

Serves 8–10

This is a delicious dessert served with a fresh fruit sauce, such as a raspberry coulis, and plain sponge fingers.

600 ml (1 pint) milk
6 egg yolks
100 g (4 oz) caster sugar
2 teaspoons cornflour
300 ml (½ pint) double cream
a few drops of vanilla extract or essence

Heat the milk in a pan over a medium heat. In a bowl, beat the egg yolks until pale and fluffy. Mix together the sugar and cornflour and add to the yolks, beating thoroughly. Pour on the hot milk. Return the mixture to the pan and, over a very low heat and stirring all the time, bring just to the boil. Allow to simmer for 2 minutes. Remove the pan from the heat and leave to cool, stirring occasionally to prevent a skin forming.

Whip the cream, add the vanilla extract or essence and fold into the custard. Pour the mixture into a 1·2-litre (2-pint) container and freeze for 4–6 hours (whipping twice during the freezing time to prevent large crystals forming) until firm.

Vanilla Ice Cream

Traditional ice cream is made with a base of cooked custard enriched and lightened by the addition of whipped cream. It is vastly superior to the lazy method using a base of raw eggs, which is a parfait rather than a traditional ice cream. This, the traditional recipe, does require whipping once or twice during freezing.

25 g (1 oz) cornflour
600 ml (1 pint) creamy milk, or a mixture of half milk
and half cream
4 egg yolks
100 g (4 oz) caster sugar
a few drops of vanilla extract or essence
450 ml (15 fl oz) double cream, whipped

Mix the cornflour with 2 tablespoons of the milk or milk and cream. Heat the remaining milk or milk and cream in a pan. Add the cornflour paste to the pan and, stirring constantly, cook until it is thick.

Remove the pan from the heat and beat in the egg yolks and sugar. Return the pan to the stove, lower the heat and cook until the mixture thickens. Cook for a further 2–3 minutes. Remove the pan from the heat and cool, stirring occasionally to prevent a skin forming.

When cold, add the vanilla extract or essence, fold in the cream, pour into a container and freeze for 1–2 hours. Remove from the freezer and mix gently to prevent large crystals forming. Return to the freezer. Repeat this process once or twice more during the next 3–4 hours of freezing, or until the mixture is firm and no large ice crystals remain.

Coffee Ice Cream

Serves 8–10

The best ever coffee ice cream!

175 g (6 oz) coffee beans
300 ml (½ pint) creamy milk, or a mixture of half milk
and half cream
25 g (1 oz) cornflour
300 ml (½ pint) single cream
4 egg yolks, beaten
100 g (4 oz) granulated sugar
600 ml (1 pint) double cream, whipped

Roughly crush the coffee beans in a pestle and mortar, or place them between layers of greaseproof paper and bruise and crush them with a hammer or rolling pin.

Heat the milk or milk and cream mixture in a pan, add the crushed coffee beans and leave, near the heat, to infuse for 20 minutes. Strain and discard the beans.

Mix the cornflour with 2 tablespoons of the coffee-flavoured milk. In a pan, heat the remaining coffee-flavoured milk and the single cream together. Add the cornflour mixture and, stirring continuously, cook over a low heat until thick. Cook for a further 2–3 minutes. Add the egg yolks and sugar and cook again until thick. Cook for a further 2–3 minutes. Remove the pan from the heat and cool, stirring occasionally to prevent a skin forming.

When cold, fold in the whipped cream. Pour the mixture into a container and freeze for 4–6 hours, stirring thoroughly after the first hour and removing once or twice more from the freezer for further thorough stirring, until the mixture is firm all through and no large ice crystals have formed.

Chocolate Ice Cream

This is a classic, rich chocolate ice cream.

25 g (1 oz) cornflour
300 ml (½ pint) creamy milk, or a mixture of half milk
and half cream
4 egg yolks, beaten
250 g (8 oz) plain dark chocolate, broken into pieces
450 ml (15 fl oz) double cream, whipped

Mix the cornflour with 2 tablespoons of the milk or milk and cream. Heat the remaining milk or milk and cream in a pan. Add the cornflour paste to the pan and, stirring constantly, cook until it is thick.

Remove the pan from the heat and beat in the egg yolks. Return the pan to the stove, lower the heat and cook until the mixture thickens. Cook for a further 2–3 minutes. Remove the pan from the heat, add the chocolate pieces and stir until melted. Cool, stirring to prevent a skin forming.

When cold, fold in the whipped cream, pour into a container and freeze. After an hour, remove from the freezer and stir gently. Return to the freezer and freeze for a further 4–6 hours, or until firm.

Chocolate Roll

Serves 8–10

Do not avoid this recipe because a *roulade* is difficult to roll up, the joy of this one is that the chocolate roll is frozen and then covered with cream and sprinkled with grated chocolate, so any mistakes are well hidden!

2 tablespoons fresh orange juice
225 g (8 oz) plain dark chocolate, broken into pieces
3 eggs, separated
75 g (3 oz) caster sugar
1 quantity chocolate ice cream (opposite), softened slightly
300 ml (½ pint) double cream
1 tablespoon dark rum
50 g (2 oz) dark chocolate, grated

Line a 20 × 30 cm (8- × 12-inch) swiss roll tin with bakewell paper. Preheat the oven to Gas Mark 5/190°C/375°F.

Heat the orange juice in a pan, add the chocolate and stir over a low heat until melted. Beat together the egg yolks and sugar until light and fluffy. Whisk the whites to soft peaks. Stir the yolks into the chocolate mixture and fold in the whites. Pour the mixture into the lined swiss roll tin and bake in the oven for 15 minutes or until firm to the touch. Leave it to cool in the tin.

When almost cold, turn out on to a clean tea towel and spread with the ice cream. Quickly roll up, place on a serving dish and freeze for an hour.

Whip the cream with the rum and spread it over the roll. Sprinkle over the grated chocolate. Leave to soften slightly for 20–30 minutes before serving.

Cheesecake

Serves 8–10

A light and delicious cooked cheesecake.

150 g (5 oz) digestive biscuits, crushed
1 teaspoon ground cinnamon
50 g (2 oz) butter, melted
50 g (2 oz) cornflour, plus 2 teaspoons
210 ml (7 fl oz) milk
4 egg yolks, beaten
450 g (1 lb) curd cheese
100 g (4 oz) granulated sugar
2 teaspoons grated lemon rind
a few drops of vanilla extract or essence
150 ml (¼ pint) thick greek yogurt
150 ml (¼ pint) double cream, whipped

Preheat the oven to Gas Mark 2/150°C/300°F.

Mix together the crushed biscuits, cinnamon and melted butter, and press into a 22 cm (9-inch) tart tin with a removable base.

Mix together the 2 teaspoons of cornflour and the milk, add the egg yolks and, over a very low heat, stirring constantly, cook until thick. Cook for a further 2–3 minutes, remove the pan from the heat and cool.

In a food processor or electric mixer blend together the curd cheese, sugar, lemon rind and vanilla extract or essence. Add the remaining 50 g (2 oz) of cornflour and the yogurt and blend again. Add the cooled egg mixture and blend well. Fold in the whipped cream and pour over the biscuit base.

Place the cheesecake on a baking sheet and bake in the oven for 2–2½ hours until firm in the middle. Turn off the heat and allow the cheesecake to cool in the oven.

Honey and Walnut Cake

Serves 8–10

A rich, nutty cake to keep a day or two before using and to serve with a fresh orange salad or fruit salad.

225 g (8 oz) clear honey
6 eggs, separated
100 g (4 oz) self-raising flour, sifted
100 g (4 oz) ground walnuts
2 teaspoons grated orange rind
1 tablespoon orange flower water
icing sugar to dust

Line a 20 × 7 cm (8- × 3-inch) deep cake tin or soufflé dish with parchment paper. Preheat the oven to Gas Mark 4/180°C/350°F.

Melt the honey in a pan over a low heat. Beat the egg yolks until fluffy; then pour in the warm honey, beating all the while. Fold in the flour and nuts; then the orange rind and orange flower water. Beat the egg whites until stiff and fold in.

Pour the mixture into the prepared cake tin or soufflé dish and bake in the oven for 30–40 minutes or until firm in the centre. Leave to cool in the tin. Turn out when cold, wrap and store. Dust with icing sugar before serving with cream.

—5—

SAUCES, DRESSINGS AND DRINKS

We have become accustomed to using raw egg in many of our finest classic sauces. It seems impossible that an acceptable mayonnaise can be made using hard-boiled egg yolks, and even more unlikely that a hollandaise or béarnaise sauce can work just as well with hard-boiled egg yolks as with raw ones. In fact, the mixture is easy to handle, tastes wonderful and is less likely to curdle while keeping warm in a *bain marie* than the classic raw egg yolk version.

There seem to be as many, if not more, delicious sauces to be made using hard-boiled eggs than ever there were with raw eggs. There is also no more messing about with egg whites and last-minute debating about whether to store them or throw them away. The hard-cooked egg white can be chopped and added to salads, soups or, in some cases, to the sauce itself.

In the classic versions of sauces such as hollandaise and béarnaise, the binding of the sauce is traditionally produced by cooking the raw egg yolks very slowly. In these recipes the egg yolks are, of course, already cooked and it is simply a matter of emulsifying the cooked egg yolks with the other ingredients. The end result is also every bit as good – or better – and almost indistinguishable from the generally accepted method.

The secret of many of these sauces is to sieve the cooked egg yolks very finely, purée them in a blender, or pulverise them in a mortar with a pestle.

This selection includes hot and cold sauces, dressings for salads, dressings for meat, fish and vegetable dishes, and sweet sauces for puddings and desserts.

Mayonnaise I

Makes 180–210 ml (6–7 fl oz)

If carefully and correctly made this mayonnaise is almost indistinguishable from the classic mayonnaise made with raw egg yolks. It is easiest to make in a food processor, but it can be made by hand if the egg yolks are pressed through a fine sieve first. Make sure all the ingredients are at room temperature for making it.

4 hard-boiled egg yolks
1 tablespoon white wine vinegar
4 tablespoons olive oil
4 tablespoons sunflower oil
1 teaspoon Dijon mustard
salt and pepper

Blend the egg yolks until smooth in a food processor. Add 1–2 teaspoons of the vinegar then, gradually, drop by drop, add the oils just as you would if making a mayonnaise using raw egg yolks. As the yolks begin to absorb the oil you can increase the speed of the flow, but be careful, it can still curdle. Add the mustard, the rest of the vinegar, and salt and pepper to taste. It can be stored for up to 24 hours in the fridge, in which case it should be left at room temperature for 2 hours before serving (add 1–2 teaspoons of hot water if it separates).

NOTE
If the mayonnaise is too thick, add up to 1 tablespoon of water, milk or thin yogurt, very gradually!

Mayonnaise II

This is a much lighter version and good with cold fish dishes. It is especially appreciated by those who find a classic mayonnaise too rich.

4 hard-boiled egg yolks
4 tablespoons olive or sunflower oil
2 tablespoons milk
4 tablespoons thick greek yogurt
1–2 teaspoons Dijon mustard
salt and pepper

Blend the egg yolks in a food processor until smooth; then add the oil, drop by drop. When all the oil has been incorporated, slowly add the milk, and then add the yogurt. Add the mustard and season to taste. This mayonnaise will keep for 3–4 days in a screw-topped jar in the fridge.

Egg and Garlic Dressing

Makes about 180 ml (6 fl oz)

This is like a very light and delicate mayonnaise, excellent as a substitute for the classic garlic mayonnaise – *aïoli* – that accompanies the fish soups of southern France. Use this in the same way or serve it with cold chicken or shellfish.

2 hard-boiled egg yolks
180 ml (6 fl oz) thick greek yogurt
4 tablespoons olive oil
1–2 garlic cloves, crushed
salt and pepper

Blend the egg yolks in a food processor (or press through a sieve). Gradually add the yogurt and olive oil. Lastly add the garlic, and a little salt and pepper.

Cover the mixture and place in the fridge for 1–2 hours for the flavours to blend and mellow before serving. Use immediately.

Mayonnaise III

Not a true mayonnaise, as it contains no oil, but a delicious dressing for coleslaw and other winter salads.

4 hard-boiled egg yolks
4 tablespoons milk
4 tablespoons double cream
180 ml (6 fl oz) thick greek yogurt
1 tablespoon mild mustard
salt and pepper

Blend the egg yolks in a food processor or press through a sieve; then gradually add the milk, cream and yogurt. Add the mustard and salt and pepper to taste, and beat well. Use as soon as possible.

VARIATION
Add a further 2 tablespoons of thick greek yogurt to this mayonnaise and you have a superb sauce.

A Whole Egg Sauce

Makes about 240 ml (8 fl oz)

This is a favourite sauce of mine, good with meats, fish or vegetables; excellent with cauliflower.

2 hard-boiled eggs, chopped finely
2 tablespoons white wine vinegar
6 tablespoons olive or sunflower oil
1 tablespoon finely chopped capers
1 tablespoon finely chopped onion
freshly ground black pepper

Blend all the ingredients together in a small bowl. To serve, mix well and spoon over meat or vegetables, or serve separately. Use at once.

Egg, Yogurt and Onion Dressing

Makes about 240 ml (8 fl oz)

This is a very light dressing, good with salads and hot or cold hard-boiled eggs; also excellent poured over baked potatoes, rice or pasta.

2 hard-boiled egg yolks
240 ml (8 fl oz) thick greek yogurt
4 spring onions, chopped finely
salt and pepper

Blend the yolks in a food processor (or press through a sieve). Gradually add the yogurt, and then add the spring onions and seasoning. Use as soon as possible.

Horseradish Sauce

Makes about 350 ml (12 fl oz)
Serves 4–6

Try this sweet, sharp sauce with plenty of bite with hot cooked
beetroot as a winter vegetable, or with Jerusalem artichokes.

15 g (½ oz) butter
1 small eating apple, peeled and grated
1 teaspoon grated onion
2 hard-boiled egg yolks, sieved
2 teaspoons grated horseradish
1 teaspoon cornflour
1 tablespoon milk
240 ml (8 fl oz) natural yogurt
salt and pepper

Melt the butter in a saucepan, add the apple and onion and cook
over a gentle heat for 3–5 minutes. Remove the pan from the
heat and stir in the egg yolks and horseradish.

Mix the cornflour and milk to a smooth cream, add to the egg
mixture and return the pan to the stove. Cook over a gentle heat,
stirring, until the mixture thickens; then simmer for 1–2 minutes.
Remove from the heat, add the yogurt and salt and pepper to
taste, stir well and gently reheat. Serve at once.

Smetana or Soured Cream Sauce

Makes about 420 ml (14 fl oz)
Serves 6–8

This light, smooth sauce is excellent with fish, such as plaice, cod or smoked halibut; it is also good with pork dishes.

2 teaspoons cornflour
1 teaspoon water
2 egg yolks, beaten
1 tablespoon granulated sugar
2 teaspoons Dijon mustard
300 ml (½ pint) smetana or soured cream
2 tablespoons white wine vinegar
1 tablespoon chopped fresh chives
salt and pepper

In a medium-size bowl mix the cornflour and water to a smooth paste, add the egg yolks and beat thoroughly. Add the sugar, mustard and smetana or soured cream and mix well.

Pour the mixture into a saucepan, place over a low heat and, stirring continuously, bring to the boil. Simmer for 1–2 minutes, remove the pan from the heat and cool slightly. Add the vinegar, chives and salt and pepper to taste. Serve at once.

Quick Lemon Sauce

Makes about 240 ml (8 fl oz)
Serves 4–6

This is a lovely sauce and very easy to make. Serve with fish, such as plaice or sole, or try it on vegetables like broccoli or spinach.

grated rind of 1 lemon
175 ml (6 fl oz) double cream
2 hard-boiled egg yolks, sieved
2 tablespoons thick greek yogurt
1 tablespoon lemon juice
a pinch of ground mace
salt and pepper

Put the lemon rind and cream in a saucepan and heat gently over a low heat. Remove from the heat and leave to infuse for 3–4 minutes; then strain and return to the pan. Add the egg yolks, yogurt, lemon juice and mace and seasoning to taste, and mix well. Reheat over a low heat, but do not allow to boil. Serve at once.

Hollandaise Sauce

Makes about 420 ml (14 fl oz)
Serves 6–8

Making a hollandaise with hard-boiled egg yolks and melted butter works wonderfully well, though it needs the same care and attention to prevent curdling as the classic version. It is easiest to make in a blender and then to pour it into a double saucepan, or bowl over a pan of hot (not boiling) water, where it can be kept warm until needed.

5 hard-boiled egg yolks
6 tablespoons warm water
250 g (8 oz) butter, melted
2 tablespoons lemon juice
salt and pepper

Place the egg yolks in the blender and blend until smooth. Gradually add the warm water and mix to a cream. Then, drop by drop (as for mayonnaise) add the warm, melted butter until it has all been incorporated. Place the mixture in a bowl over a pan of hot water, or in a double saucepan, and heat gently. Add the lemon juice and season with salt and pepper to taste.

Béarnaise Sauce

Makes about 480 ml (16 fl oz)
Serves 6–8

This classic French sauce adapts very well to being made with
hard-boiled egg yolks. The delicious flavour comes from the use
of dry white wine, tarragon vinegar and fresh herbs. Make this
sauce in a blender, and ensure that the wine and vinegar mixture
and the melted butter are warm when added to the hard-boiled
egg yolks.

6 tablespoons dry white wine
6 tablespoons tarragon vinegar
½ shallot, chopped
2 teaspoons chopped and 1 sprig of fresh tarragon
4 white peppercorns
250 g (8 oz) butter
5 hard-boiled egg yolks
2 teaspoons chopped fresh chervil
salt and pepper

Put the wine, vinegar, shallot, the sprig of tarragon, peppercorns
and 25 g (1 oz) of the butter in a saucepan. Bring to the boil and
boil until reduced by half; strain the liquid and keep it warm.

Melt the remaining butter over a low heat.

Purée the egg yolks in a blender, and gradually add the wine
mixture to make a thick cream. Then slowly, drop by drop,
incorporate the melted butter. When all the butter has been
added to the egg yolk mixture, pour it into a bowl placed over a
pan of hot water or into a double boiler to warm through. Add
the chopped herbs and season, if necessary. Serve the sauce
warm, not hot.

Orange and Lemon Sauce

Makes about 300 ml (½ pint)
Serves 6–7

A superb sauce for all seasons: try it with baked apples in autumn, chilled strawberries in summer, and mince pies at Christmas.

grated rind and juice of 1 lemon
grated rind and juice of 1 orange
2 teaspoons cornflour
1 tablespoon water
2 tablespoons granulated sugar
2 egg yolks, beaten
50 g (2 oz) butter, cut into pieces
2 tablespoons brandy
2 tablespoons Cointreau
2 tablespoons double cream

Place the rind and juice of the lemon and orange in a saucepan and heat gently. Mix the cornflour and water together, and stir into the fruit juice. Add the sugar and cook until thick. Remove the pan from the heat. Pour in the egg yolks and mix well. Return the pan to the heat and cook until just simmering; then simmer for 1–2 minutes, stirring continuously. Strain the sauce and return it to the pan. Add the butter, brandy and Cointreau and gently reheat to melt the butter. Remove the pan from the heat, add the cream and serve at once.

Custard Sauce

Makes about 480 ml (16 fl oz)
Serves 4–6

This can be used to fill trifles. It is also delicious poured over stewed fruit, summer pudding or steamed sponge pudding.

1 teaspoon cornflour
1 tablespoon granulated sugar
480 ml (16 fl oz) creamy milk
2 egg yolks, beaten
a few drops of vanilla extract or essence
a few drops of almond extract or essence

Mix the cornflour and sugar together, add one tablespoon of the milk and mix to a smooth cream. Add the beaten egg yolks. Heat the remaining milk and pour over the egg and cornflour mixture. Return the mixture to the pan and, over a very low heat, while stirring constantly, bring *just* to boiling point; then simmer very gently for 2–3 minutes. Cool slightly and add the vanilla and almond extract or essence. Serve hot or cold.

Foaming Egg Sauce

Makes 480–600 ml (16–20 fl oz)
Serves 5–8

This sauce makes an excellent substitute for that classic Italian sauce, Zabaglione. It is good with steamed pudding, or serve it on its own in individual glasses with sponge finger biscuits.

1 teaspoon grated orange rind
180 ml (6 fl oz) white wine, plus 1 tablespoon
2 tablespoons granulated sugar
2 tablespoons cornflour
2 eggs
180 ml (6 fl oz) double cream, whipped

Combine the orange rind and the 180 ml (6 fl oz) of white wine in a saucepan and place over a low heat. Mix the sugar and cornflour with the tablespoon of wine and stir in the warm wine. Return the mixture to the pan and cook until it begins to thicken. Whip the eggs until thick and fluffy and pour into the pan. Cook slowly over a low heat and simmer for 2–3 minutes, stirring continuously. Remove the pan from the heat, strain the sauce and cool.

Just before serving, fold in the whipped cream. Serve immediately.

Lemon Curd

This lemon curd keeps well in the fridge. It is useful for filling tarts and can be used in desserts and creams.

grated rind and juice of 2 lemons
1 tablespoon cornflour
2 tablespoons water
180 g (6 oz) granulated sugar
5 egg yolks, beaten
50 g (2 oz) butter, cut into pieces

Put the lemon rind and juice in a saucepan. Mix the cornflour and water together and stir into the lemon juice. Cook over a low heat until the mixture begins to thicken, stirring constantly. Add the sugar, egg yolks and butter. Cook over a low heat, stirring constantly, until the mixture is really thick. Cook for a further 3–5 minutes; then remove the pan from the heat. Pour the curd into clean, dry jars and cool.

Cover when cold and store in the fridge. It keeps for 2–3 weeks.

Egg Nog

2 teaspoons cornflour
2 teaspoons granulated sugar
2 tablespoons milk
3 egg yolks, beaten
150 ml (¼ pint) single cream
150 ml (¼ pint) brandy
150 ml (¼ pint) double cream, whipped
a little grated nutmeg to dust (optional)

Mix the cornflour, sugar and milk to a smooth paste; then add the egg yolks.

Heat the single cream in a saucepan and, when almost boiling, pour in the egg mixture. Stirring continuously, cook over a gentle heat until the mixture begins to thicken. Continue cooking for a further 3–4 minutes. Remove the pan from the heat, cool slightly and add the brandy. Leave to cool.

When cold, fold in the whipped cream and chill. Serve dusted with a little nutmeg, if wished.

NOTE

If wished, this can be stored for 12–24 hours in the fridge, in which case the whipped cream should be added just before serving.

INDEX

Ice cream, chocolate 76
  coffee 75
  vanilla 74

Leek and egg tart 51
Lemon, cheesecake 78
  chiffon layer 66
  cold syllabub queen 65
  curd 93
  marshmallow mousse 67
  sauce, orange and 90
  sauce, quick 87
  soufflé 59
Lentil eggs 41
Lettuce and butter omelette 33
Lime tart 60

Maple syrup cream 72
Mayonnaise, I 81
  II 82
  III 83
Middle Eastern eggah and courgettes 35
Mousse, chocolate marquise cream 68
  egg 52
  lemon marshmallow 67
Mushroom, gratin, egg and 48
  hard-boiled eggs with 43
  topping, egg and potato pancakes
    with 39
Mustard sauce 43

Omelette, cheese 26
  and herb butter 32
  lettuce and butter 33
  Middle Eastern eggah and courgettes
    35
  Spanish 34
Orange, custard 62
  and lemon sauce 90

Pancakes, egg and potato, with
    mushroom topping 39
Pastry, shortcrust 9
Pâté, egg 17
  egg and tuna fish 16
Pears, buttered, in vanilla sauce 57
Pickled eggs 19
Pie, egg and onion 50
Prawn mould, egg and 53

Quick lemon sauce 87

Red peppers, eggs with 36
Rhubarb tansy, a 63
Rum cream and chocolate mould 70

Salad, egg and avocado 30
  egg and caviar 23
  starter, smoked trout and egg 22
Savoury eggs 46
Scrambled eggs and watercress sauce 24
Shortcrust pastry 9
Smetana or soured cream sauce 86
Smoked salmon stuffed eggs 21
Smoked trout and egg salad starter 22
Soufflé, lemon 59
Soup, cold cucumber 13
  curry 15
  egg and garlic 12
  egg and herb 11
  spinach 14
Spanish omelette 34
Spinach, sauce, eggs in 31
  soup 14
  supper, egg and 42
Sponge cake 9
Storing eggs 6
Syllabub queen, cold 65

Tart, leek and egg 51
  lime 60
Tomato, bake, egg and 45
  sauce 47

Vanilla, ice cream 74
  sauce, buttered pears in 57
Very simple starter, a 16

Whole egg sauce, a 84